—— THE ——

Awakening Cantos

Rick Gardner

PAGE PUBLISHING
Conneaut Lake, PA

First originally published by Page Publishing 2024

ISBN 979-8-89315-834-2 (pbk)
ISBN 979-8-89315-851-9 (digital)

Printed in the United States of America

The Awakening

A dark road, I am blind
Yet see the trees
Roam as given
Travel with faith

Find a path to love
The path is clear
Give to those around you
As they need you

Journeys change
Go back to yours
Go forward as needed
Never sure or how
The journey is yours only

The mystery of joy
Nature tells us we are one together
Survive, thrive, live strong

You die alone, you live to teach
Give happiness, peace of mind,
Forgiveness
Understand others
Find the star in each soul
As it is not hidden

Long lines in the ground disappear
With time
As all of us do
There is no real time
Nor eternity
Only now

Bright skies, be light, envelope, elevate, climb
There is no darkness

On your travels see the good
The beauty around you
The wonder that God gave us
Creation, existence

We are not alone
Give to those around you
As they give to you

Stories never end, they are forever
They are forever endless
Always changing
You are the story

What trail do you follow
Go alone in the forest
See, smell the flowers
Walk in peace

Behind questions are answers
We don't understand now
Maybe never

Exist on finding happiness in one life
children, friends, most important family
Be happy

We are given a chance to help ourselves and others
Which course do you choose?
Follow your bliss, it is a gift
This is it
The moment now is a heavenly awakening

Looking Inward

Transcend your feelings of guilt
Be free of them
They are only destructive
It takes time to face the grim truths
Living in the past is only hurtful

See Eden in your own world
The kingdom of our father
Spread before you
Yet we do not see it
Open eyes make the world beautiful
See God everywhere
In everything around you

Arrival in Heaven is where you already are
Enjoy the present
Look around
The amazing universe is obvious

Life is difficult to truly understand
Origins are not clear
The end results are everywhere
Will change
Time and pressure always win
Except this reality

Be willing to adapt to change
Everything changes for the better
Not in our control
History is not kind
Life will continue

Look deeply at every event
Life exists for a reason
Why? We cannot fathom
Hope for our survival
It is not guaranteed

Challenge those around you to be honest
Difficult but necessary
Trust is necessary for any relationship to survive
In all religious beliefs
The well-being of families

Doubt has its own reason to exist
Something only humans can experience
Concept of failure
Children will eventually ask
Why they are here, what they are, what the future
will be
Am I OK?

Open your mind
Meditate on your well-being
Internalize. Time becomes an ally
Live life to its best

Enlightenment is found in the light
Not found through escape
Learn limitations
Accept them

Looking Outward

Enjoy life, exist with nature
No choice, no option, no problem
Surrounds each, offers comfort
Relief to our daily struggles
No compensation is asked for

See the life around you
Complex interactions abound
Different species compete to survive
Expand your territorial holdings
Reproduce at costs
Things change, extinction happens
Conflict creates trials of strength

Fear of failure is profound
Penetrates your mind, endless
Some want you to fail

Children need constant attention
Must love them, nurture them

Accept their daily needs
They are our future
Eventually our caretakers
Be patient, caring
Teaching the importance of knowledge

Introspection

Hope is an internal dilemma
We all want to believe all is well
Believing all will be well
Nothing wrong will happen
Sometimes defying the real world

Our existence
Brought about by mere chance
Adapting to pressures
Never-ending environmental changes
Elemental creation
Chemical bonds
Structural alignments
Nuclear organization, evolving biologic relationships

Entropy rules energy and mass
Disorder is necessary and inevitable
Rules of chemical reactions are given
Do not change
The ultimate results do though

All life is dependent on reproducing itself
Time and external pressures cannot be defeated
The need to create, reproducing yourself
Self-evident for generational survival
Ingrained in every life-form
Unexplained adaptation

Pressure surrounds everything
No escape, constant, unforgiving
Must be redirected
Becomes destructive

Sex and reproduction defines life
Necessary for evolution
Complete the genetic expression
Given one, day one

No life-form can exist without reproducing itself
All life-forms are here
from the grace of God
Roll the dice, let it flow

Trapped by necessity and desire
All succumb
God wins
Believe in yourself, thank yourself

Complete your journey
See the heaven in those around you
Feel the karma in all

Deep Thinking

Always lost then found
Our thoughts create feelings
Being alone
We seek approval from others
Regardless of their true role in our lives
Judgment is present
Perceptions of life matter

Believe in being regenerated
To be a complete human
Become an example for others to follow
Respect, becoming whole
A difficult challenge
Internal peace is difficult
Simple for some
Impossible for others

Best to love everything about yourself
Comfort with those around you
Past, present, future

Loving relationships should be unbreakable
Sadly fail occasionally
Emotions dominate reason
Revenge dominates the outcome
Separation the only result

Introspection is a necessary exercise
Look at your own existence
Are you comfortable with relationships
Continue, be satisfied in your own world

Are you mentally stable
An easy question within ourself
Nobody else can answer this
Outwardly presentable
Inwardly hidden

Judgments of your behavior
Thoughts good and bad
Closed minds never open
Closed to everything, unable to open

Move on with life
No other option is acceptable
Join the world that surrounds you
Give in to the feeling of astonishment

Captivating your very being
Difficult for some
Impossible for many

Obstacles exist and multiply easily
Always present
A state of confusion, unpredictable

The Beginning

When does life start
The end is clear
Look in the mirror
See yourself as you really are

Childhood should be a happy existence
Sadly not always true
Sometimes hateful
Difficulties can start on day one
Expectations are present
Continue forever
Succeed or succumb

Growing up is not a choice
Learning not an option
Listen and learn
Every sentience, every equation
Teaches a certain knowledge
Hidden in its structure

Knowledge is a reflection
Of your internal experiences

We all grow with someone's help
With their direction
No chance to change this definitive relationship
Family structures dictate outcomes
Good or bad
You are not alone

Hopefully finding others to help
Change your direction
Possible destruction
Parental love is ultimately important
No other choice possible

Taking care of yourself is not an option
Look inside, be critical, enjoy the ride
It eventually ends

Those you love change
Some leave
Some just go away to love others
There are others to love

Our lives change since we were born
Our mothers
created comfort, care
Enveloping you with their love
Giving direction and needed nutrition
Next up, hold on

Questions

Do you really want to read this?
My wife says stop writing
It doesn't make sense
Hard to ponder

Am I happy, am I productive?
Do I give comfort to others?
Families are a necessary responsibility
Need to protect them
Gladly accepted, your definitive job
Nothing else is acceptable
The return is apparent

Have I reached a sense of accomplishment?
Sometimes doubtful, difficult to accept
Be satisfied with a successful outcome
Be impressive

Where am I? Only here today
Maybe different tomorrow

Who knows? Things change
Change for the better?
Unknown outcomes

Do others respect me? Love me?
Respect my past accomplishments?
Time will tell, you already know the answers
Hopefully our family sees us as we are
The need to create a life to enjoy
Have you created a positive joyful existence?

No question should go unanswered
Why do I exist?
Be silly at times, be funny
Make people laugh
Sometimes with you
Sometimes because of you
A child enjoying your presence
Is one of the great joys in life
Nothing comes close

Nobody knows what is next, time will tell

The Next Last Supper, Not Over Yet

We all face a last supper
In the end a last of everything
Sacrifice to those around you
Give grace and advice
Be thankful, pray, be quiet
Reflective, you gave direction
How to live
Already written, will be painted, revered

See the heaven you gave to others in need
Understanding their true being
Try to serve them
Before your end as they served you
We live in a dangerous world
Children give us direction, responsibilities
A gift to the future
Nature's way of giving you a way to follow

Give redemption, forgive their sins
Sermonize as you feel necessary

They may not listen
Do you care in your final days?

Your family, friends need comfort
Speak openly
Tell of your joys
Children need to hear your voice
Hopefully teaching we live in an unknown world
Expectations never ending
Learn and repent
Your Lord is watching

Eat, praise, the table is set
Some will deny your presence
No future, be served with reverence
Expect what will happen next
God directs the outcome

Finding peacefulness
We are only actors in a play
Conflicting thoughts
This maybe the last time I exist
The ending will not be fruitful
Definitely painful
Pray for your redemption

Hell exists only if you let it to become part of you
Deny its existence
Life is and always a gift
Eat, drink, talk as this is your Last Supper
Give yourself to all
You will be resurrected soon, forgive all
God has given, gift, life, growth, love, family
Sons and daughters to teach, blessed by all
Thank God I am alive

We arise in prayers by family
Living in their thoughts, missed
Brought back to life again and again
Never ending

Unsure of the true message
Just out of reach
Hidden inside, walk alone, quiet, no sounds
Solitude, peacefulness, no words spoken, no thoughts
Silence is everywhere
Thank you, Lord, be alone, nobody else is needed
Only once but with a peaceful smile
Peace exists in quietness
Listen to the Lord around you
Lives begin, are lost in a short time

No looking back, teaching yourself, difficult but given
Finding joy in all things, Thank God for our life

Need to enjoy the forest
God created a lovely world
Look see the wonders
All religions teach us how to treat our fellow beings
How to behave, how to treat each
Jesus, the Koran, Judaism/Moses, Buddha, Tao, Hindu
Follow them
Humans quarrel, fight, kill each other
Never ends, why?
The Tower of Babel exists in thought and action

Pray endlessly, hope for redemption
God speaks to all endlessly
Best to listen and follow

See the pure face of true life around
Vibrant colors, sounds, feelings
Enjoy the taste of life
Possibly your last supper
Give love to those around you
Celebrate their presence at the table
Give grace to all, everyday

Directed by God's ultimate direction
Give and take, Expect betrayal
Many forms of a Judas surrounds us
Hidden but painfully present
Waiting patiently to destroy beliefs
Must defend and defeat

We are not alone
Give to those around you
As they give to you
The past is over, the future never ends
It is always endless
God rules, always has
The path is clear, see the light
Respect yourself, be all, give all, be true
You know the way
Go back to where you started
Hard to believe a child is in you
Waiting to hope, dream, pray, grow
Families expect no less
Be an example for others to follow

A since of a peaceful ending is necessary
Not easily found
Death offers a release
A chance to be one with your maker, be reborn

Have you given yourself to others?
Last thoughts dominate, say goodbye
I will be back one way or another

Being Alone

Given a chance to explore inside
Not always pleasant
Feeling isolated, unloved, ignored
Deep separation from others
No clear path ahead, some darkness, isolation
Conflicting thoughts

Explore those around you
They can offer comfort, direction
Lost in time, hoping for resolution
Finding absolution

Giving release from expectations
Examine your depths, looking beyond others beliefs
Be one in your own self
Achieving greatness
No looking back, nothing lasts
Give yourself to others, time, love

Our touch gives comfort, giving care
All need your love
As you need their love
Love yourself
Spread your love to all

In the end, we are all alone
A happy child is within you
Give all, be true, dream, pray, hope
Never go back, Resurrect yourself

Waiting to Die

Listen, death speaks to you
All journeys end, sometimes difficult to see
Life ends for all, seek comfort, seek touch
Wait slowly, let go slowly, spread your love
Your family needs to see relief, say farewell

Sing a song, loud as you can
Make others cry
Tears offer a peaceful goodbye
Thankful you gave their love

Contentment, relaxation, accepting God's judgment
Good, bad, or indifferent
A path already defined
A peaceful, painless end is best
A relentless doubt will persist
Give yourself to your Lord, go quietly

The Joy of Living

Look, see the world surrounds everything
Colors, life, sounds, visions

Joy is hidden deeply inside
Growing, expanding
Not difficult to find, it is there to behold
Feel it, offer it, experience it
Gives back to all

Be part of creation, take my hand
Close your eyes, feel those around you
Inside is lost, at times never found
Look up, see the wonder
Stars are there, find them around you
Encircling you, capturing your very existence

Day one, close the doors, open the windows
The view is wonderful
Let go, stop thinking

Be alive, then die in peace
Happens to all living things
Escape from your day, give love, joy

Live to Believe

God shows, knows all, taught all
See, look, give all, everywhere
We are one together, created as one
No division, equality for all beliefs
Give yourself to all, they await

Hope, give comfort to others in need
Sadly everywhere, seeing them
Unable to save, God knows what will happen
Fate has dictated the outcome
Hard to change
The ending is in your heart
In your hands

The future is given, deny or change the results
Best to forget and live today
Be satisfied, seek fulfillment, life has been a gift
Believe and know God is in you

Be alive, exist in harmony, create harmony
Spread your love, we need your love
Give life, accept life, it surrounds us
Inside a real being exists
Given strength and direction
Every human is given hope
A chance to live, believe
Thankful for all
The surrounding world, family, friends

Life ultimately involves death in many forms
All life dies at some time
Lost every day, some pain in each

Find the truth, it is obvious
Look, see, touch everything
Be alive, look down, around
The earth welcomes you
Plant yourself, grow, offer yourself
Get your hands dirty
Dig deep, deeper, no need to stop
Find the end, live underground
Become quiet, escape, become one
With the ground around you

Arise in time, back to light
See everything, feel everything
Be glad you truly exist
Become the God within your being
Look inside, find what is hidden
Deep inside you know yourself

One tells all, the beginning, the end
Become a teacher, a prophet
Give resolution to all
Pray for peace to all

The End of Nothing

Endless thoughts
Nothing exists for long
Doomed to disappear
Eventually gone, no evidence of existence
Traceless, gone from eternity, lost forever
Emptiness, hidden, closeness
Closed for others to see
Lost in the depths, dark, deep

Find the magic that surrounds us
Basic wilderness, everywhere
Nature is there, never lost
We live in a wonderful world
Given to ours by God, creation
Show others how to live
Expand their own lives
Everyone's beliefs, light
May be extinguished at some time

Why wait for the end? It will happen
As everything dies
Nothing can change this truth
We are given a choice
Enjoy life or deny it
God offers nothing, only a chance to give

Time will end for all
We are given a choice
Enjoy life or deny it
God offers nothing, only a chance to give
Nothing will or can change
The outcome is given, accept, move on

Find a peace of mind, no other choice
Endlessly a challenge
Hidden inside, need to be found

See the end of everything, live now
Or die in the depths of self-recrimination

What I Love

How do you define love?
Deep unknown feelings
Sometimes uncertain, questioning
A deep sense of giving and receiving

A need we all want, desire
At times consuming, changing
Something you feel deep inside
Be consumed by love, live to enjoy

Mothers know, fathers learn
Children need our love
Even before their birth
Becoming one inside, not knowing
Able to learn, children know when they exist
Needing love, given life

Smile, laugh, cry, grow
It is what is meant to be

For all, in all, all of us
Love the simple fact of being alive
Love yourself and all others

Day of the Dawn

The sky explodes, the sun appears
A single star in the universe, created
Giving life, evolution, creation
A future to behold

Another day, be awake
See the sky around you
Beauty everywhere, wonder
Thankful you exist, were born
Give yourself, be light, belief of life
Dawned before

Arise, see the sun going down
Feel the greatness our God has given
Feel the sunshine in your face

Only One

Being one, a fact of life
No one else around
Feels good, isolation
Absolute quietness if necessary

No words, be yourself
No one to worry about
No one to answer to

Become one, look inside
A complete individual exists there
Thinking as one
Striving to be one

God is one, look inside
A complete individual exists there
Thinking as one
Striving to be one

God is one, believe, teach
There is only one

One next day to enjoy
Better than one last day
Perform, comfort
Look and see one world

Each and every one needs someone
That will listen, enjoy talking, acting, playing
Being themselves, one seeing nothing else
Enjoy being alone
It is yours, no others around
Feels good, nature is there
One entity, always present

One life to live, from day one
Give to others, free to offer your love
Returns are given

One universe, one God
Combined together, never ending
Only one outcome

Your World

The world speaks to you, sees you
Sounds surrounds us
Just listen and enjoy
Sights, wind, the moon, distant stars
Time existed before our beginning

Light travels in space
Directed by our Maker
Never ending, created
Nature needs care, feel it inside of you

We are one in this world
Grow, give, accept time
It ends, but is endless

Try to expand your world
Difficult to do
Something to create

Belong to this world, no others
Simple joy in its existence
God shows why, created once

We are a small part of all things
One life, give what you may
Say what you may, others are listening
Just speak, your words are giving, sincere, teaching

Sisters, brothers know
Hopefully seeing the future
A universe everywhere
Behold, look upward
Never down

Giving your love creates the ultimate joy
To yourself, family, friends
Move to a higher level
Stand above, alone at times
Share, carry each, forgive
Give love to one and all

Creation

All life started, created by God
Millions and millions of years
Some life died, extinguished
Only to be replaced by others
Humans could be next
Existence is time limited
Universal happenings dictate the outcome

Become your own creation
Create children, care them, direct them
Enjoy every child's presence
Become the teacher
Preach how to become whole

Create everything, write, sing, play
Be with nature around
Listen to the wind, birds singing, wolves growling
What is said is heard
Think about the joy you create

We all seek comfort, love, attention
You are given choices
Believe you are created for a reason
Given a chance to be completely in love
Your family knows you created greatness
A gift to the future

Dreams

Sleep, dream, give in, expand
Exist for a reason, enjoy the simple trip
Does not last for long, changing with time

Sometimes a gift, sometimes frightening
Difficult to understand the meaning
Hidden inside, seems real
They become forgotten, difficult to remember
Create questions

Life could not exist without dreams
Dream daily when awake
Tell others of your thoughts
Dreaming helps, gives freedom, enjoyment

See, feel, accept the end of dreams
They will disappear, a sad ending, gone forever
A new awakening happens, a new world

Dreams tell us what is next in our lives
What we truly want to happen
Time alone, time with loved ones
Time with friends, a time to think
A time to die in peace

Dream of tomorrow
Enjoy the show, awake with a smile
Say thanks I am alive, the end has to wait
Dream again and again till the end

Hidden Thoughts

Desire, what does it really mean?
Why do we feel this need?
Deeply wanting satisfaction, enjoyment, gratification
No need to ask what else

The need to find a peace of mind
Your God, your savior, your lover
Missing days of mindlessness
No worries, just enjoying the moment
Flying, soaring, being alone, being together

Seeking fulfillment, learning of your needs, not theirs
Inside we only need ourselves
How? Now look beyond
Answers are clear, definite
They may become apparent at some time

May not like what is there
Past behavior may haunt you

Move on to today, forget
Past offenses are gone

Discover what makes you happy
Let the child in you use the day
Allow the feeling, enjoy
Your loved ones, a lover can expand your life
Given daily

Enjoy the moment given to you
Endless, give in to your desires

Listen, Learn

Many speak, say little
Hear less, only themselves
Alone, hidden inside
Learning nothing

Never learned how
A closed mind, closed to all
Never truly listening
Hidden in themselves

Listen, look, learn
Learn when not to speak

Learn how to change
Listen to your heart
Tells you how to feel real
Has been there before
Sadly not listened to
Only denied
Try to listen to the sound of rain on leaves
Creates wonder

Truly

Why are we not true to ourselves?
Taught to ignore others
Not able to change
Truly captured, lost

What is true?
How to answer this
Changes in each
Never real to all

The universe is true
Nature is true
We are not
A sobering thought

Many ignore each other
Their truths are the only one
Never changing
Dies with them

Today, Tomorrow

Both exist, cannot be denied
Death the only other option
Live today, look for tomorrow
Give yourself, enjoy yourself

Those who love you, give themselves
Understand your needs, wants
Expect the same from you
Deep inside we know how

Live every day the best you can
Hope tomorrow will be better
Hell is with us, deny its existence

Be willing to die
Sacrifice yourself, die in bliss
Your Lord accepts your gifts

Fly Away

Be one with the sky
Look down, the real world is there
Behold its greatness
God gave us all
Children, family, loves to enjoy
Give back, fly above
The sky is yours, behold

See the light in all
It is not hidden
Needs to be found, followed
Your future awaits
Your life is now
Fly with birds
God gave them wings
God gave us the sky

Where to Go

Be a lover, be a friend, be a teacher
Be one with nature
Follow your Lord, you know the way
Give to all, hard for some, simple for many
There is one God, one Allah
The one for all, peace be within you
Believe, rejoice, give yourself to others
Care, create greatness, give comfort
That is all that is asked of you

Lost Angels

I saw them once, felt them
Now gone hidden, disappeared
Possibly forever, sent to tempt you
Now only a memory

Left thoughts of forgiveness, mercy
Hard to believe they existed at all
Wanting more, desiring more
Unsure what was taught
What was true

Lost at times, seeking guidance
Hidden inside, sometimes dark
Sometimes enlightening
Not understanding the message
My role unknown, contemplating
Who I am, why I am

In times of need, they are there
Following you, will be with you

Forgotten Memories

Some good, some bad
Only you know
Wishing some disappeared
Forever gone, lost in the wind
Sadly deep inside, hidden
Down memory lane

We enjoy memories
The first hug, the first kiss
The first love, deeply held inside

Your mother's kind words
Your father's direction
Your friends and struggles

Never forget where you came from
It is inside you

Night

Day and night cannot exist alone
The sun disappears, night arises
Darkness pervades everywhere
Sometimes brings joy and love
Nature's way of telling you to hide
Love those in the comfort of dark
Solitude, closeness, passion at times

Night has existed since time began
Became on day one
Begins as the day ends
Slowly encompassing, expanding
The galaxies show themselves

Comfort and joy to some
Death and destruction to others
Hopefully brings sleep, peace, dreams

Close your eyes, start dreaming
Darkness surrounds, quietness

Given and wanted
Night and day since time began
Given to all, directed by God

The Circle of Life

Connected, seen in all directions
Obviously even sometimes misunderstood
Returns with a deepness
A great vision

The Healing Circle exists in all
We are all one together
Black Elk saw, then spoke
Speaks of being connected, living with all
Taught what to see
The world around everything, every human
Ongoing life and death, we are all one together
One with nature, each day
Giving trees, water, the sky, seasons, creation

Paths to create, paths to follow
Become one with your own
You are the circle of life
Circles surround all life

The circle ends, life ends, begins again
I am ending, eventually just a memory
The next circle of life starts
Circle yourself with those who love you
Give yourself to the circle of life

Finding Happiness

Difficult thought
Never truly found
Gone at times, found at times
Wishing it existed for all

Not given to many, missing in most
A journey not defined
For many never found
Life creates drama, fear of being

What creates being happy?
There is no true definition
Each decides, give to others
Try to define its real existence
It is hidden inside you
Defines you every day

The real happy is the smile
In a child's face

Roads Not Traveled

Travel with pride, with a purpose
You know where to go
Which way is best

Learning where to go, not to go
Unsure why
Choices made, loves lost
Some found, some gained

Life continues for all
Eventually ends for all
Look, see, accept, move on

One road, one path
Will change
Never clear where to follow
Never a clear choice
One goes down, one goes forward
You will not know which one
They all end at the same time

Be young again, be the child in you
Take the road ahead of you
Getting old is not a choice
A road we all face, look ahead
Get lost, find your own road

Old Friends

Some are gone, some stay forever
Growing together
Finding, growing, remembering
Ending in time, gone

Feel them, believe in them
Feel them inside you
They live in you
They are you

Show your real self, be proud
Something to believe in
Walk with them, dance with them
Dance away
Close your eyes, see them as they were

Gave their love at times, freely
Some do now
Hard to say we are allowed to have loving
Relationships at times

Felt good, feels good
Doesn't it, circles back

Some become the love of your life
Young love, a friend forever
God's gift, a lover and a friend
Then children as it was meant to

Goodbye to Past Loves

To all my loves, I say goodbye
They are in my mind, hidden
Forgotten but endlessly remembered
Never leaving, deep inside
Thank you for being there
I needed you, you gave yourself
Hope you felt the same

Gave joy, satisfaction
An endless lover gone away
Sad but true, found another
A definitive need
Thank God for giving them to you
The joy of the act was meant to be
Hold me again, I remember, miss you
Hopefully so do you, goodbye

To Light

Open, see, the way is hard
From dark to light
Not knowing the path ahead
What is light meant to be
A gift to you from God
Lives in you, shows to others
Expresses, brightness, your loves
See it in your eyes
Crystal clear, you know your light
Always was and will be

Dark beliefs destroy
Entrap everything, everyone
A child brings life
Was always meant to be
Brings joy, a path to lightness
Follow them, learn from them
Become the light for others to see

I Am Alone

Everyone is alone
Born as one, lived as one
Alone in your thoughts
Sometimes existing alone

Strange feelings, only inside yourself
Nobody knows why, unable to express
Or understand
You are one and alone at times
Best to live with this
Being alone is your choice.

Are You Alive

The path is obvious
Where to go, be alive
Live to be one who knows
You need to explore, grow, teach

Find those in the dark
They want and desire direction
Give your life, create life
Do you know where to go?

Inside you are one, alive
The child in you knows, God knows
Hidden inside you
Known only to you, seeing you

Do not asks why
Pain is your only option
Live to survive, be alive
Love those around you, they are alive

Why Not Now

All need to give themselves
Not tomorrow but now
All see you as you are
God tells you who you are
What and how to treat each other
Other lives, other creatures
We all need each, need the surrounding world
God is in everything you see
Feel it, live it, enjoy it

Now is the time to open your mind
To everything, find reason to live
Your Lord gives you a choice
Be alone or together with the world around you
Look inside you
There is a God waiting to be found
Touch your inner peace
Touch those around you
Feel their inner joy of life
They need you as you need them

Mothers

We all need them, loved by them
Could never have existed without them
God's gift, God's demand to follow
Bring Eve to life or die
Maybe the snake and apple were meant to be
Who really knows?

Can't live with them
Can't live without them
They rule our existence

No man exists without a mother
God gave men his reason to live
A woman to enjoy
A woman to provide joy and the future
A mother to be one again

Motherhood is a gift from God to all life
Mother Earth is real
Always was and will be
What your mother taught you is the truth

Daughters

They consume you, listen closely
Challenge you, they know you
It is their job, you are next to give in
Mothers to be, God gave them for a reason, to rule
Need to listen or fear the result
Fathers gave them their life

Only to give them to others
Life cannot exist without them
At times, thank God they leave you alone

Teaching all, becoming all
Able to defeat all
Just wait, see what happens
Listen and learn, they teach

They know what is next
Sons will need them, other daughters to guide them
To give them joy, provide for them

Give care and attention
Children are next, demanding you
Learn it is best to just give in

Anger, Why?

Feel the flower's bloom, tree's blossom
Nature is not angry, we are at times
Angry at each other, no reason

Enjoy to give yourself, become the tree
Become the flower, anger is not nature's way
Leaves eventually fall, seasons begin and end

Anger can last forever, deeply inside
Becomes self-fulfilling, self-propagating
Leaves no option to become hateful
Consumes you, occupies you, destroys you

Become the flower, the tree
Forget, leave anger behind
You will forget why, listen, change
Your true nature denies anger
Hate, anger is only destructive

Better to be the falling leaf

Jesus Calls You

Hold on, Jesus comes calling
Telling you where to go
Where to be to be, what to be
Always in you, deep inside you

Will be in you for your life, hold on tightly
Sees you as you are
One with God, your Lord speaks to you
Loves you as you are, teaching you

Began the day you were born
Brought to life as a gift
Began in all
Your daily struggles will never end,
They exist in you, his thoughts are you
Give yourself to those you love
To all that need your love
Jesus showed and told how to love each
He is there, just look and see
He comes to you in many forms

Showed me what to be, made me
Taught me how to become awake
How to be fruitful, thankful

God Gave Me a Reason

God gives and takes you to unknown places
Gave a reason to live
A son to die for
Sons and daughters for all to die for

A reason to enjoy life
A reason to find love
Reason we are here

Deep inside we are all blessed
Given birth, given a way to provide to those we love

Give yourself to your Lord
The words are the same in any language
Give up your anger at others
God says peace to all
Say good night
Tomorrow will amaze you, just wait

The End of My Canto

Amazingly, I survived all of this.

About the Author

Rick Gardner, Doctor of Veterinary Medicine, having taken an oath to protect all animals, his duty to God and nature. He is not sure where these words came from, but as he reflected, there came a need to express himself. Every animal taught him something, gave him words, beliefs. He never takes death lightly. God gave him a reason to save lives, to perform at his best at all times.